How Monkeys Make Chocolate

Foods and medicines
from the rainforests

by
Adrian
Forsyth

OWL BOOKS

Owl Books are published by Greey de Pencier Books Inc., 179 John Street,
Suite 500, Toronto, Ontario M5T 3G5

OWL and the Owl colophon are trademarks of Owl Communications.
Greey de Pencier Books Inc. is a licensed user of trademarks of Owl Communications.

Distributed in the United States by Firefly Books (U.S.) Inc.,
230 Fifth Avenue, Suite 1607, New York, NY 10001.

This book was published with the generous support of the Canada Council,
the Ontario Arts Council and the Government of Ontario through the
Ontario Publishing Centre.

Canadian Cataloguing in Publication Data

Forsyth, Adrian
How monkeys make chocolate

Includes index.
ISBN 1-895688-45-0 (bound). — ISBN 1-895688-32-9 (pbk.)

1. Wild plants, Edible – Juvenile literature.
2. Wild foods – Juvenile literature. 3. Medicinal
plants – Juvenile literature. I. Title.

QK98.5.A1F67 1995   j581.6'3   C94-932489-2

Design & Art Direction: Mary Opper

Photo Credits: Front cover, John Pontier/Animals, Animals; pp. 5 Frans
Lanting/Minden Pictures; 6 right, S.J. Krasemann/DRK Photo; 6 left, 7, Mark Plotkin;
9 Andre Baertschi; 9 inset left, Frans Lanting/Minden Photos; 9 inset top, Wolfgang
Bayer; 10 N.H. Dan Cheatham/DRK Photo; 11 left, Mark Plotkin; 11 right, Haroldo
Castro; 12 top, Chocolate Association; 12 bottom, J.E. Simmons; 13 National
Geographic Society; 14 N.H. Dan Cheatham/DRK Photo; 15 left, L. Emmons; 15 right,
Mark Plotkin; 16 Michael Fogden/DRK Photo; 17 Russel A. Mittermeier; 17 inset left,
Mark Plotkin; 19 S. Nielsen/DRK Photo; 20 Russel A. Mittermeier; 21, 22 left and
right, Adrian Forsyth; 23 left and right, Barbara Zimmerman; 24 Richard K. La
Val/Animals,Animals; 25 Sydney Thomson/Earth Scenes; 26 Adrian Forsyth; 27 D.
Cavagnaro/DRK Photo; 28 Adrian Forsyth; 29 Scott Camazine; 31 and inset, Adrian
Forsyth; 32 top and bottom, 33 and inset, Haroldo Castro; 34 left, S. Nielsen/DRK
Photo; 34 right, Mark Plotkin; 35 Larry Ulrich/DRK Photo; 36 Russel A. Mittermeier;
37, Adrian Forsyth; 37 inset, Ted London; 39 and inset, 40, 41, 42, 43 and inset,
Andre Baertschi; 44, 45 Michael and Patricia Fogden; 46 Haroldo Castro; 47 Andre
Baertschi; back cover, Adrian Forsyth

Printed in Hong Kong

A   B   C   D   E   F

CONTENTS

Rainforest MYSTERIES

The rugged mountains of Indonesian New Guinea make up a great tropical wilderness, one of the last left on our planet. Blanketed with unbroken rainforest, it is home to tiny, widely scattered villages. The Hatam people who live there use the forest every day for food, for medicine, for their houses, for the bows and spears they use to hunt and fish. The Hatam are forest experts. They know what no scientist knows — how to live in and make full use of a rainforest.

In the time I spent with the Hatam, I was amazed at the way they could make a fire in pouring rain, build a camp in minutes or find a bird's nest full of eggs if they were hungry. Travelling through the forest, I constantly asked my Hatam guides about the plants we saw. There was never a plant they didn't know. Both adults and children could tell exactly which kinds of fruits were sweet and which were bitter and what sort of birds preferred them. Everyone knew the sort of palms to cut for salad, and recognized which vines held sap fit to drink and which ones could be used to make strong rope.

On one hike I noticed a part of a beetle, just a tiny piece of its mouth parts. I showed the fragment to my guides and asked if they recognized it. The next day their children brought me a whole bag full of insects, each one the same kind of metallic-green stag beetle. The mouths of the beetles exactly matched the piece I had found.

The Segama River in Borneo winds through a forest rich in beauty and in life. Every forest holds its own mysteries.

People have found many uses for rainforest plants and animals. Stinkbugs (near left) can be a nutritious snack, high in protein and full of flavor. This rosy periwinkle plant (upper left) from Madagascar can make a medicine to treat cancer.

Not only did the Hatam know exactly which beetle I wanted to see, they also knew what plant it ate and where that plant lived. When they found I was interested in insects, they began pointing out the ones I could eat. I was surprised to learn that they relished large black stinkbugs. Found as pests in gardens all over the world, stinkbugs are called that for obvious reasons. But despite their pungent odor they have a crunch and an almond flavor that the Hatam enjoy.

Rainforest dwellers have a deep understanding of their forests that took them hundreds or even thousands of years to build. The wild plants the Hatam rely on can't be found in gardens, and their seeds aren't sold in stores. Little of what they know has been written down. Rainforest wisdom and forests themselves are both threatened by a busy, hungry world that is fast turning wilderness into plywood and farm fields.

No two of the world's rainforests are alike. Each has its own set of plants and animals. The forests of New Guinea, rich in wild nutmeg trees and giant pigeons, aren't like the forests of Borneo that are home to wild mangoes and orangutans, and these in turn differ from west African forests with kola trees and chimpanzees, and the forests of South and Central America with papaya trees and spider monkeys.

This book is about the amazing relationships between the plants and animals and people of the rainforests. People like the Hatam depend directly on the forest for everything they need. And relationships in living forests are just as important to you and me, giving us spices, cosmetics, foods, drinks, materials and medicines. Every time you eat chocolate or take an aspirin, you are sampling a tiny bit of forest life.

We are just beginning to understand the richness of rain-forests: what tastes or poisons or cures hide in every leaf, which insects depend on each variety of plant, which fruits feed birds and which feed bats or monkeys. We are just starting to appreciate the mysterious thing we call a forest.

Ethnobotanists like Mark Plotkin (at left) study how people who live in the rainforest use plants for medicine. This shaman or medicine man (at right) of the Tirios people of Surinam possesses knowledge that is vanishing along with the forest.

How Monkeys Make Chocolate

The Manu River is born in the snowy peaks of the Andes Mountains of Peru. It runs steeply downhill until it suddenly meets the Amazon rainforest. There the landscape flattens out and the river slows as it meanders through the wild and ancient forest. Gigantic fig, cedar and kapok trees stand along the river. Some of these trees are as wide as a house at their base, and they spread a huge green canopy of leaves high in the air. But here and there the majestic scene is disturbed by a commotion.

The forests of Manu are full of monkeys. Capuchin monkeys and spider monkeys, very strong and intelligent, travel through the forest in large troops. They jump from tree to tree, crashing through the vegetation in search of food. Groups of tiny, agile squirrel monkeys often follow in their wake, swinging and chattering. They poke through the debris scattered by the larger monkeys, eating the insects their movements shake from their hiding places. There is safety in numbers — the more monkeys, the more eyes to spot predators. The squirrel monkeys get easier access to food and, without the constant need to watch for enemies, the capuchins can spend more time searching for fruit, seed pods, palm nuts and insects to eat.

The forest of the Rio Manu is home to thousands of plants and animals, and is one of the most diverse rainforests on Earth. A brown capuchin monkey (inset left) uses its keen eyes, powerful jaws and nimble hands to find and eat a great variety of foods. Squirrel monkeys (inset above) join troops of capuchins on food-finding trips through the forest.

Fruit-eating monkeys are especially eager to find one small, inconspicuous tree. As I travelled through the forest, I hardly noticed it myself, except when it sent out its strange fruits. The fruits grow right out of the trunk and branches of the tree and ripen into long, orange pods. The first time I examined a pod, I wondered what could open such a solid fruit — it was almost as big as a football and definitely too tough for most birds to eat. But it wasn't long before I saw which animals are smart and strong enough to get into the pods.

The brown capuchin monkeys were clearly excited when they found ripe pods, chattering noisily and leaping around. I watched as they pulled the pods loose and used a two-handed smash, pounding them against branches to break them open. Then they eagerly ate the contents of the pods. I did as the monkeys did and smashed a pod

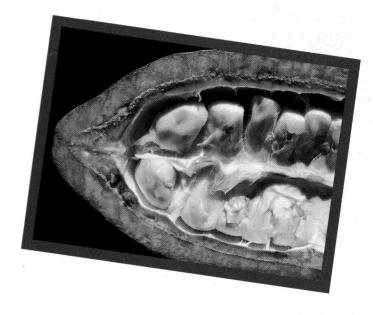

against a tree. The broken pod revealed several rows of seeds the size of large beans, each one coated with a glistening white coating. I took a taste, sucking the pulp off a seed. The pulp was sweet, juicy and delicious, especially after a sweaty hike through the forest.

But the seeds inside were another matter. I broke one open and nibbled. The inside of the seed was rich brown and tasted like unsweetened cocoa powder. And that's what it is: the monkeys had found the cacao tree, and cocoa is made from its seeds. The taste of the seeds was horribly bitter after the sweet pulp, so again I followed the monkey's actions and just spat them out as I walked along. This is how cacao trees are spread through the forest. Without monkeys to take the fruit and scatter the seeds, most of the pods would just fall into the shade of the tree and rot.

When the monkeys introduced me to the cacao tree, I was amazed at how perfectly the fruit works. The strong pod protects the seeds while they are ripening, and then it changes to a bright color to attract monkeys when ripe. Since the pods grow right out of the trunk and branches, they are easy for monkeys to reach. The cacao tree rewards the monkey's effort with sweet pulp, a food so tasty that a monkey with a pod will tear off through the forest to keep stronger monkeys from stealing it. To make sure that the monkey eats only the pulp and spits out the seed, the seeds contain bitter chemicals.

The relationship between cacao and monkeys has existed for millions of years. Just a few thousand years ago, humans began to value this plant. Perhaps the first people to enjoy the fruit of the cacao discovered it the same way I did, by watching monkeys. Eventually, we learned to enjoy the strange taste inside the cocoa seeds, which we call cocoa beans because of their shape.

Cocoa beans are the main ingredient in chocolate, possibly the most delicious flavor humans have yet discovered. But a lot of work goes into turning the fat, bitter cocoa beans into sweet, smooth candy. Roasted cocoa beans are heated and ground into a dark paste that is called chocolate liquor, even though it doesn't contain any alcohol. Very high pressure separates the chocolate liquor into cocoa powder and a thick, golden liquid called cocoa butter. Pure chocolate candy is made from chocolate liquor, with sugar to sweeten it and extra cocoa butter to enrich it.

Costa Rica is one of the places where people grow and process cocoa. Ripe pods (left) can range in color from green through yellow and orange to deep red. As the cocoa beans (below left) are removed from the pods, cleaned and dried, they turn dark brown.

People in Mexico today make chocolate much the same way their ancestors did. They drink bowls of frothy sweetened chocolate to celebrate happy occasions.

I once helped make chocolate from scratch. Alcides, a farmer living in west Ecuador, was tending a small patch of cacao trees near the section of rainforest where I was working. I helped him collect several bushels of yellow pods and together we piled them on the forest floor. Piling the pods seemed to heat them, which made them finish ripening. The pods were opened and the seeds spread out to dry. We roasted the dry seeds and ground them smooth, mixing them with raw brown cane sugar and a dash of cinnamon and vanilla. This mixture was heated with just enough water to make a thick paste. We rolled up the paste in aluminum foil and let it cool and harden into a solid, dark brown roll. Shavings of this chocolate scraped into a mug of hot water made a delicious rich-smelling drink topped with an oily layer of melted cocoa butter.

Some people drink cocoa without sugar. The Mayan people in Central America add hot pepper and drink it as a fiery, bitter brew. But most people, like monkeys, are repelled by the strong taste of cocoa beans, especially if they have just eaten the sweet pulp.

This Costa Rican woman might enjoy some of the sweet pulp as she harvests the coffee crop. Once the seeds are cleaned, dried and roasted, we buy them as coffee beans, either whole or ground.

What gives cocoa beans their taste is a combination of more than 750 natural chemicals. This unique formula is what makes chocolate taste like chocolate, and the complicated mixture of rich and bitter tastes might explain why chocolate-lovers rarely tire of their favorite flavor.

One of the bitter ingredients in cocoa is caffeine, a chemical that stimulates the nervous system in humans and other animals. Caffeine protects plants from being eaten, since it is bitter and also acts as an insecticide. Caffeine also makes people feel awake and energetic. We learned to like caffeine and started to grow many of the plants that contain it — we harvest cacao seeds, tea leaves, the kola nuts used to make cola drinks and, of course, coffee seeds.

Coffee comes from a small tree that grows wild in Africa. We now grow coffee throughout the tropics, on plantations at the edges of mountain rainforests. In the wild, when coffee shrubs are heavily laden with bright red fruits, flocks of noisy nervous parakeets swarm over them. The birds rapidly shell the coffee fruits, swallow the pulp and discard the bean-shaped seeds. I learned to imitate them, to enjoy the slippery, sweet pulp coating the seeds and to spit out the seeds without chewing. Parakeets and people spread coffee seeds.

Chimpanzees do the same thing for kola seeds. They eat the fruit and drop the seed where it can sprout into a new tree. We use the hard kola seed, called a nut, to add caffeine and flavor to soft drinks. If monkeys make chocolate possible by scattering cocoa seeds, then chimpanzees make cola drinks by planting kola.

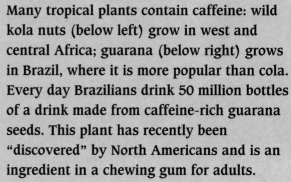

Many tropical plants contain caffeine: wild kola nuts (below left) grow in west and central Africa; guarana (below right) grows in Brazil, where it is more popular than cola. Every day Brazilians drink 50 million bottles of a drink made from caffeine-rich guarana seeds. This plant has recently been "discovered" by North Americans and is an ingredient in a chewing gum for adults.

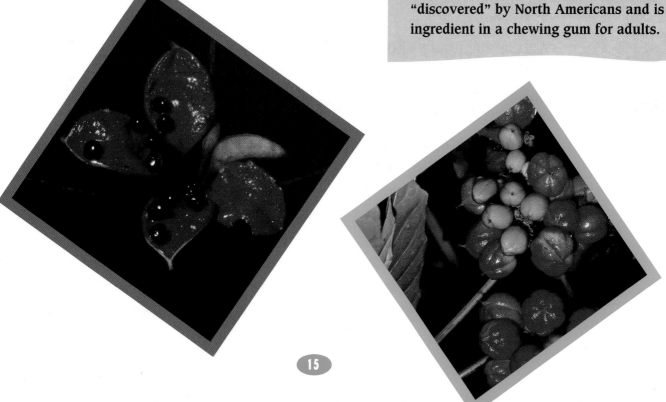

The study of rainforest animals can lead to surprising discoveries. Poisons found in the venom of snakes like the eyelash viper of Costa Rica (left) are used to make medicine to control blood pressure in people. We can even learn about plants by watching what animals do. Monkeys enjoy cupuaçu fruit (inset opposite) and people have learned to eat it fresh or make it into juice. The woolly monkey of the Amazon rainforest (opposite) knows which leaves are nutritious and which are full of toxins.

Many rainforest plants are well known where they grow but nowhere else. My favorite Brazilian fruit is a close relative of cacao, and is called cupuaçu. People like it for the same reason monkeys do — the sweet, creamy white coating around its seeds. The seeds are thrown away and the light clean flavor of the pulp makes a popular ice cream or delicious drinks that are perfect on a steamy tropical afternoon. You probably have never tasted cupuaçu, since it is rarely sold outside of markets in the Amazon.

The pulp that covers the seeds of cocoa, coffee and cupuaçu is sweet and naturally appealing to monkeys and humans alike. But the bitter seeds are valued world-wide, because of the caffeine in them. I imagine that people began using cocoa and coffee to relieve tiredness and headaches, and wild cocoa beans are still used medicinally by some native peoples of the Amazon. Strong, bitter substances, such as the caffeine found in coffee and the tannins found in tea, are important in traditional medicines all over the world.

People aren't the only ones to use plants as medicine. Chimpanzees have been found chewing on rough, bitter plants that have little nutritional value but that contain chemicals that get rid of parasites. Leaf-eating monkeys sometimes eat mildly toxic leaves to cure themselves of stomach troubles. Some birds weave antibiotic

grasses into their nests to prevent the growth of bacteria that might cause sickness. Native North American people have watched bears dig up and roll on roots and bulbs to fight insects and fungus in their fur.

We still know very little about thousands of kinds of rainforest plants and animals. We don't even have names for many of them. But what goes on between all the plants and animals is what makes the forest work — flowers are pollinated, seeds are spread, animals are fed. Little by little, we are learning to see and to use these connections. Without the relationship between monkeys and cacao, we would not have chocolate. And living forests are full of riches yet to be found.

Why Cherries Are Red

To me, few sights are more appetizing than a bowl full of ripe, red cherries. Cherries are my favorite fruit, and the cherry trees in my garden near Washington, DC, produce plenty of them. Unfortunately, I almost never get to eat any. The birds beat me to it.

As soon as the fruit begins to show the first signs of ripening, flocks of robins, grosbeaks, scarlet tanagers, northern orioles and mockingbirds descend noisily on the trees. These birds are excellent cherry pickers. Soon, hardly a single cherry has escaped their attention and appetite, and my trees are almost bare of fruit.

It's easy to see that the birds relish the sweet red fruit, but watch carefully and you'll also see that it's good for a cherry tree to attract birds. When a bird flies off with a ripe cherry in its beak, it swallows the flesh of the fruit and is left with the seed at the center. Cherry seeds are hard and indigestible — in fact, they are called stones — so the bird throws the seed away. Cherry seeds are carried to new locations as far from the parent tree as the birds fly, in just the same way that cocoa seeds are scattered by monkeys throughout a tropical forest. Some of the seeds from the cherry trees in my garden will sprout and turn into new trees, which is why the trees produce seeds and cherries in the first place.

Red berries and fruits have bright pigment and sweet sugars that attract birds like this bohemian waxwing. The male holds up the fruit to impress a mate.

Heavy-billed caciques wait for papayas to change from green to orange before they eat the fruit and scatter the ripe seeds through the tropical forest.

Fruits such as cherries are a living sign language, a way for the plant to communicate with the animals that live nearby. One of the things I enjoy doing when I walk in a forest is trying to "read" the messages sent by the fruits I see. I ask myself what animal the fruit attracts with its special color, shape, size, scent and taste.

Cherries attract birds in a simple and obvious way. They turn from green to red. Birds are the best way for cherry trees to get their seeds scattered, so the ripe fruit has bright color instead of, say, a sweet smell to attract them. Birds have a weak sense of smell but, along with a few animals such as coral reef fish and some mammals such as monkeys, they have color vision equal to ours. So birds and humans alike see bright color as the sign of ripening in fruit.

It's easy and tasty to test the ripeness of most fruits and berries. Compare a sour bite of a green hard fruit with the sweet taste of one that is soft and has changed to a more intense color like red, orange or purple. These changes are no accident. The fruits and berries we see today are "designed" by evolution. They look and grow the way they do because their survival depends on being picked by the right animal as soon as they are ripe.

When it comes to ripeness, timing is everything. Inside an unripe fruit, the seed coat is often soft, so it cannot protect the seed inside if an animal swallows or chews it. But when a cherry is red, its seed and the nutrients it needs to sprout are protected by a hard coating. Some fruits make very sure that animals don't eat them until their seeds are ripe and ready to be planted. Unripe papayas are not only hard and unappetizing — they're poisonous! As a papaya ripens, it turns from green to orange, and its flesh changes from a bitter, hard mass laced with toxic sap to a soft pulp rich in sugars.

My cherries in Washington ripen in the summer, but seasons in the rainforest aren't as definite. A tropical plant might have fruit at different stages of ripeness, all at the same time. The brilliant colors of fruit dotting the dark forest, in the shade of a thick layer of high-branches, are clear messages the plants provide to tell us and other animals which fruit is ready to eat.

▶
▶ Rainforest fruits like *Haemelia patens*
▶ use strong contrasting colors to stand
▶ out in the forest. Both the dull green of
▶ the unripe fruit and the deep blue-black
▶ of the ripe fruit stand out against a
▶ bright red bract or base.

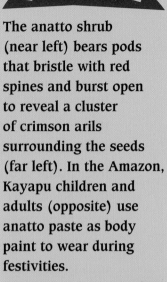

The anatto shrub (near left) bears pods that bristle with red spines and burst open to reveal a cluster of crimson arils surrounding the seeds (far left). In the Amazon, Kayapu children and adults (opposite) use anatto paste as body paint to wear during festivities.

Most of the fruits we know are like cherries, with some sort of skin holding in the sweet flesh. But many plants attract animals by surrounding their seeds with a brightly colored, oily pulp called an aril. In these fruits, a heavy-walled pod splits open when ripe to reveal the brilliant aril that holds the seeds.

In the tropics, anatto bushes grow wild along the Amazon, and many people grow it in their gardens. Hungry birds are attracted to the bright color of anatto arils, and so are people, but not for food. Throughout the Amazon basin, the native people use the oily aril to paint their faces and bodies. Anatto arils are also used to make other cosmetics — anatto dye is what makes some lipsticks red — or to add color to foods such as margarine and rice.

We value anatto aril because of its color, but the oil it contains also makes it a rich food source. An oily aril provides energy that birds can store in their bodies, long-lasting nutrition to add to the instant energy they get from sugary fruits. Plants with arils ripen throughout the year in tropical forests, and fruit-eating birds depend on a constant supply of arils and fruits to survive. In the northern forests of Canada and the United States, there are only a few plants with arils, such as bittersweet vines and prickly ash. Here, most birds include insects in their diet because fruit is not always available.

Some arils are highly flavorful. The arils around nutmeg seeds are dried to make the spice called mace, which gives its special flavor to pumpkin pie and other desserts. In the rainforest, large fruit pigeons swallow the nutmeg seed and its surrounding aril whole. The bird's soft stomach removes the aril without damaging the seed. The nutmeg seed is then regurgitated, undamaged and ready to sprout. The seeds are indigestible and will poison animals that chew and eat them. But humans make use of the part of the plant that is poisonous to other animals. Not only are we much larger than fruit pigeons, but we can also control the amount of the nutmeg seed we eat. Ground and sprinkled on food as a spice, nutmeg's sharp taste livens up bland foods. We can safely use a small amount of nutmeg, even though a whole seed is enough to make a person very ill.

Instead of bright colors, some plants use smells to attract animals. The night air of the rainforest is full of scents "speaking to" nocturnal mammals that use their noses more than their eyes.

Working for many years in forests has taught me to follow my nose, too. Once I was walking along a beach on the Pacific coast of Costa Rica, where forest met sea and sand in a vine-tangled wall of vegetation. One of the vines was an orchid with creamy white flowers and long, skinny seed pods. When I reached up and picked a pod, a sweetly familiar perfume arose. I had found the vanilla orchid, one of the most inviting scents of a tropical forest.

The fragrant vanilla pod held a mystery. Why would it have a scent? Most orchid seed pods ripen into dry, odorless casings that split open and release millions of dust-like seeds onto the wind. The vanilla pods were fleshy and packed with sticky, perfumed seeds. I looked to the pods still on the vine for clues. Many of the rubbery green pods had been gnawed by sharp teeth, yet were dangling high above the ground. Only one animal could have done this — a bat!

Vanilla orchids appeal to a bat's keen sense of smell and use scent as a chemical beacon. Bats can fly, and that's how they reach the fruits of high-hanging vines. After a bat eats a pod, it flies off, excreting and scattering the undigested seeds through the forest. The delicious smell of vanilla leads the bat to food, and the bat helps the vanilla orchid move its seeds to trees where new vines can sprout and climb. Without bats and their special relationship with vanilla orchids, we wouldn't have the most popular ice-cream flavoring in the world.

Many of the sweetest scents of the rainforest, such as the smell of a ripening banana (above left) or a vanilla pod (opposite), attract bats to pollinate a plant or scatter its seeds. Pollinated vanilla flowers develop into green seed pods shaped like string beans. Ripe pods are picked and dried to sell as vanilla beans. Soaking the beans in alcohol forces out vanilla extract, which we use to flavor desserts.

Not all rainforest smells are sweet. The durian is truly awful-smelling, a huge spike-covered fruit as large as your head. It is a dull shade of brown-green, and it is hard to notice up in the tree tops — but only if you hold your nose. When it is ripe, it splits open to reveal an oily aril surrounding inedible seeds, and it lets off an incredible stench. Hotels in Asia post signs forbidding durians in the rooms because they can smell up the entire hotel. The most nauseating plane rides in my life have been through mountainous regions of Indonesia, the passengers tossing and pitching in the turbulent air while the stench of a cargo of ripe durians filled the plane. But durian fruit *tastes* wonderfully sweet, like custard. All sorts of animals, including people, have learned to love it. In the forests of Borneo, orangutans, wild pigs and even tigers follow the durian's scent to the fruit, and then spread the durian seeds far and wide.

There are other ways for plants to scatter their seeds — the shapes of the seeds or pods can work as well as colors and smells. Dandelions and milkweeds have seed fibers that catch the wind like

Amazingly, the stinky durian is a popular fruit. Durians are found wild in the forest, or are grown in home gardens, and thousands are sold in markets throughout Borneo and the rest of southeast Asia.

Where large furry animals roam on the ground, plants like burdock let their seeds hitch a ride to a new location. Burdock burrs stick just as well to clothing as they do to fur.

a kite or sail. Maple keys grow a natural propeller that twirls and spins the seed away from the tree on the slightest breeze. Touch-me-nots have seed pods with fibers that bend like a spring under pressure as they grow, until the pod pops open and the seeds burst out. One of the most ingenious of these plant mechanical devices is used by burdock. The seeds are buried in a burr, a mass of tiny hooks that snag the fur of passing mammals, who might carry the burr great distances before cleaning it off. A Swiss inventor studying burrs had a brain wave about all those little hooks. He invented a multi-purpose attachment system that uses hundreds of little hooks snagging hundreds of little loops — it's now called Velcro!

Honeybees (this page) collect nectar and pollen from flowers. In the wild, bees build huge hives (opposite) in hollow trees or holes in rocks. People all over the world keep bees so that the sweet honey is always available.

Many plants rely on animals to spread their seeds, and almost all plants need help to pollinate. When pollen is transferred from flower to flower, seeds can develop from the blossoms. Bees fit well into flowers, and some have fuzzy hairs that pick up sticky pollen — they are excellent pollinators. Flowers use nectar to attract bees, and bees turn this sweet, thin fluid into honey by evaporating the water.

Honey powers all the bees' activities. Bees feed honey to their larvae to provide the energy they need to grow. When the air is cold, bees eat honey to generate the body heat that keeps the colony warm. It can be close to freezing outside a colony and warmer than human body temperature inside. But only if the bees have honey.

Human beings have enjoyed the taste of honey for thousands of years. It is one of the best-known treats to be found in a relationship between plants and animals. Imagine how great honey must have tasted to early humans who rarely ate anything sweeter than a plant root or wild fruit. You can recapture this sensation if you have

been out hiking for many days with little food, burning lots of energy. Suddenly, anything sweet tastes incredibly delicious, because your body needs more fuel to burn. Honey tastes good because its energy-rich natural sugars stoke a hard-working human body.

Eating honey or a ripe, red cherry is a sweet way to explore the living forest. Each fruit or honey tells a story of plants and animals working together. Each is made of a unique mix of molecules, each has its own subtle perfume and complex taste. In the sweetness of honey, in the beauty of a cherry is written the work of bees and flowers, of birds and sunshine.

Bark with BITE

Not all my experiences in the rainforest have been good. Once, hiking along a mountain ridge, I came in contact with a tree that gave me one of the worst experiences of my life. After clearing a trail, I noticed my skin was starting to itch. My finger began to swell and get hot. Then my skin turned red and blistered. Within two days, I had what looked like chemical burns on my hands and legs, and patches of rotting skin were coming loose. In the rainforest, it's hard to keep wounds clean, and I was afraid that bacteria would get into the open sores. So I left to find medical help in a town on the coast.

As I recovered in town, I asked a local forester what caused my terrible infection. He told me about the oily, poisonous bark and sap of a tree called *Semecarpus magnifica*, a member of the poison ivy family. I have a strong allergy to poison ivy, which probably made my reaction to this tree even worse. The forester told me I could recognize the tree: the trunk with its bright reddish orange, flaky bark reaches high into the rainforest canopy and adds color to the dim green gloom of the forest. Before my run-in with the tree, I had hardly noticed it. But once it was described to me, I began to see it all over. Now I think of *Semecarpus magnifica* as "the orange enemy" and I make detours whenever I see one ahead of me.

Covering the rugged
mountains of Irian Jaya
(New Guinea) are the
least-explored rainforests
in the world. They are
home to hundreds of
different trees, and even
an expert would find it
hard to recognize them all.
I learned the hard way
about the *Semecarpus
magnifica* (inset) and the
poisonous chemicals in
its bark.

My enemy tree was, in fact, protecting itself against hungry animals. Monkeys, porcupines, orangutans, insects such as termites and beetles, and sap-sucking woodpeckers — all love to chew on the tender bark or crave the sweet sap a tree makes for its own nourishment. An attack by a chewing animal can kill a tree, and some trees have learned to bite back with saps that are poisonous or gummy. Humans sometimes suffer from these defenses, but we have also learned to use them.

Chicle trees use their sap to gum up the mouths of chewing animals and to repair wounds in their bark. But humans have turned the gummy sap into a fun and useful product. When sweeteners and flavors are added to the smooth, elastic chicle sap, it becomes chewing gum. Ancient Aztec and Mayan people chewed chicle gum. They also used the durable chicle wood in temple construction and ate the delicious oval, brown fruits. Today, collecting chicle gum provides jobs for people living in the rainforests of Guatemala.

For a thousand years or more, Mayan people have collected chicle sap. In Guatemala, people still go into the forests, looking for the rough, furrowed bark of a chicle tree. They follow a practice refined by their ancestors through centuries of experience, taking good care of the forest that provides everything they need. Traditionally, there must be a certain number of trees standing before the chicle sap can be harvested. Chicle collectors know how to collect sap carefully without harming the tree. The sap is cooked in a camp in the forest, then cooled and pressed into large bricks ready for sale.

The tradition of gathering chicle is ancient, maybe as old as the Mayan civilization that flourished in Central America a thousand years ago. A sap collector (this page) makes V-shaped cuts in the bark of the tree. The sap flows into a collecting bag (inset above). Men cook the white sap in a large heavy pot (opposite below), stirring it as it thickens into a gummy mass. Mayan children (opposite above) chew the chicle their fathers have collected.

Rubber sap is another example of a gummy defense. Native people in South America made slightly cooked rubber sap into water-proof bags. Now everything from car tires to running shoes to toys is made from this amazing stuff. But it all began with a rainforest tree plugging a hole in its bark.

Cut spruce and pine trees ooze a sticky sap called pitch. Native people of the North American forests have long used pitch to treat wounds, since it is loaded with antiseptic chemicals that prevent germs from invading a tree or a human wound alike. The turpentine we use to clean up after painting comes from pine gums. The fig tree has a white sap that causes the mouth and digestive system to bleed if swallowed in large quantities. But in small doses it is useful as a medicine. Rainforest dwellers use fig sap to clean out infected skin sores, and swallow a few drops of it mixed in a cup of water to kill intestinal parasites.

Pine wood (this page) drips with golden drops of pitch. In the rare remaining old-growth forests of North America, ancient pine trees bear old pitch-collecting scars. The notch on this white pine (far left) dates from 1860 and was made by native people who collected pitch to waterproof canoes. White sap from the rubber tree (near left) has thousands of uses, from waterproofing clothing to erasing pencil marks.

Each tree sap combines food energy and defense in its own special formula. Living surrounded by trees, rainforest people have found surprisingly pleasant uses for some saps. I have drunk a refreshing chalky white sap from tropical vines and trees. In eastern Indonesia, my porters, local people who help carry gear and food through the forest, often collect a pitch-like sap from dammar trees. The hardened sap burns brightly like a candle when lit, and it gives off a sweet smell like incense.

If a tree is well defended by poisonous bark, hungry animals won't even get to the sap inside. Many barks contain chemicals that can cause bark-eating animals to bleed, or that affects their hearts or nervous systems. A mouthful of bark from the cinnamon tree creates a sharp burning on the tongue that sends a bark-chewing animal running. But very small, precise amounts of a poisonous chemical can have an effect that humans want. Many spices and medicines come from poisons, but they're safe because we can carefully control the amount we use. When you eat apple pie with cinnamon's spicy tang, a tiny bit of defensive tree bark is adding the flavor to your dessert.

Dozens of kinds of tree bark are sold as traditional medicines. The bark of a tree called chinchona gave us quinine, for years the only way to cure and prevent malaria. You might recognize quinine's bitter flavor in tonic water. Another chemical in chinchona bark can control irregular heartbeat. But perhaps the most successful medicine from tree bark comes from willows. For thousands of years, people have chewed willow bark to treat pain. The pain-killer in willow bark was the basis for aspirin, the world's most widely used drug.

We're finding new medicines in tree barks closer to home. I travelled to an island off the coast of British Columbia to measure the biggest yew tree in Canada — 3.3 m (10 feet) around. Native people knew that yew bark made strong medicine. But modern foresters just burn young yew trees with the other debris left after they clear-cut a forest. Recently, biochemists and doctors took a close look at the chemicals in yew bark. They found a compound called taxol, which is now one of our strongest weapons for fighting many forms of cancer.

The more we study the thousands of trees that make up a rain-forest, the more we learn. The world contains more than 250,000 kinds of plants, but we use only 300 species regularly. I sometimes wonder if even my "orange enemy" tree has something to teach us.

Native people of North America used yew trees for bows and paddles, and to make medicine. The reddish bark of the western yew (this page) also contains a valuable drug called taxol. Whether as spices like cinnamon in Indonesia (below), or as medicines in Africa (opposite), all kinds of tree barks are sold in tropical markets.

A Hard Nut to CRACK

Wearing a hard hat seems like a good idea when ripe castaña pods fall in the rainforest. I tread nervously under the tree limbs spreading high above my head. I know that among the leaves hide castaña seed pods that are as hard as rocks and as large as grapefruits. When a pod drops from the treetops, it hits the ground with skull-cracking force. I pick up a fallen pod. A strong chop with a sharp machete opens it, revealing a cluster of large seeds. In North America, we call these seeds Brazil nuts, but castaña trees don't grow just in Brazil. All through the Amazonian rainforest, in Peru and Bolivia, these magnificent trees reach to the top of the rainforest canopy where their leaves can harvest the energy of direct tropical sunlight.

Around every castaña tree is a web of life, a whole world of plants and animals, including humans, that depend on the tree. Their leaves and blossoms are food for animals, and their broad branches support plants like orchids, ferns, vines and wild pineapples. Most important of all are the seed pods that drop like cannonballs to the dim forest floor.

The area around a
castaña tree (this page)
is scattered with gnawed-
open pods. Inside the
castaña pod (inset) are
delicious Brazil nuts.

Some animals don't wait for Brazil nut pods to fall. Blue and gold macaws eat the developing nuts while the pods are still in the tree.

Finding a pod is the easy part of the castaña harvest. And opening it is just the beginning. The castaña seed is one of the best protected I have ever seen. Inside the armor-like pod, each Brazil nut wears a rough brown shell that takes a hammer or a strong nut-cracker to open. There is a good reason for all this armor — lots of animals want to eat castaña seeds.

While the seed pods are still on the tree, they are far above the reach of many animals. But the giant parrots known as blue and gold macaws live in the trees and are especially good at getting at the unripe seeds. A macaw has a powerful bill like a pair of shears, and can cut through branches as thick as broomsticks. It easily slices open the immature pod and eats the seeds developing inside it. But macaws can attack the pods only before they are fully hardened.

Once mature castaña pods hit the ground, the only animals smart and dextrous enough to open them are rainforest rodents such as agoutis. Using long, sharp front teeth and strong jaws, an agouti chisels and scrapes its way through the tough castaña pod. When it has managed to make a small hole, it inserts an agile forepaw and fishes the seeds out one by one. Then it uses its sharp teeth again, this time as a nutcracker, before it can finally enjoy the nut. Eating castaña nuts takes a lot of work, but agoutis are persistent.

Why are castañas worth so much trouble? Animals crave these nuts because they are nutritious, rich in protein and oil. Animals need protein to build and repair the cells that make up their bodies. Meat-eating animals get protein from the bodies of their prey but animals that eat plants are lucky to find sources of protein as rich as castaña nuts. Up to two-thirds of a castaña nut is pure oil, a fuel so concentrated that you can light a nut with a match and it will burn like a candle. All that oil provides long-lasting energy, and agoutis wisely bury stores of castaña nuts to retrieve when food is scarce.

Agoutis are experts at opening Brazil nut pods. Sometimes they consume a nut on the spot, but usually they bury the nuts in hiding spots throughout the forest.

Without the strong pod to protect them, castaña nuts can be eaten by other animals. Peccaries are wild pigs that travel through the forest in large herds of up to several hundred. I followed their trails, and it looked as if someone had plowed the forest floor. Peccaries shove their snouts deep into the soil, churning it up as they amble along. Any seeds they happen on get cracked in their powerful jaws and gobbled up. To prevent the peccaries from eating all their nuts, agoutis bury them near fallen logs where the pigs find it hard to root. A large store might be wiped out all at once, so agoutis bury seeds in many locations.

It's a good thing for castaña trees that an agouti's memory is not perfect. Or an agouti might get eaten by an ocelot or jaguar before it can find all its stored nuts. Whatever the reason, many castaña seeds are never retrieved. Nicely buried, often in sheltered spots, they eventually sprout and begin growing. Decades later, a seed planted by an agouti might become a huge castaña tree, as tall as a 20-storey building, ready to flower and to produce seeds all over again.

The castaña seeds are not the only parts of the plant used by animals. Caterpillars, sloths and howler monkeys eat the fresh green leaves. After the leaves fall, they nourish snails, slugs, millipedes and mushrooms. Rain fills the empty seed pods, turning them into miniature ponds that some animals use as nurseries. Scientists recently discovered a frog in Peru that breeds *only* in castaña pods.

Even old castaña flowers provide food for rainforest animals. The soft, cream-colored blossoms, about the size of grapes, fall to the forest floor. Their scent attracts shy brocket deer, who include them as a treat in their usual diet of shrubs, leaves and bark.

Many kinds of life depend on different parts of the castaña tree. Pods that have been gnawed open by agoutis fill with rainwater (above left) and attract frogs who lay their eggs inside. Fallen castaña blossoms lie thick on the forest floor (opposite), where red brocket deer (inset opposite) can feed on them.

The group of animals that treasure castaña trees includes us. Brazil nuts from the Amazon are relished throughout the world. Most nuts we eat — almonds, hazelnuts, walnuts, pistachios, cashews and macadamia nuts — grow on plantations. But almost every castaña nut comes from wild rainforest. Castañas grow best in the wild because a castaña tree depends on other plants and animals as much as they depend on it.

As important as the animals that spread a castaña's seeds are the bees that pollinate its flowers. Rainforest bees collect pollen and nectar from all kinds of flowers. Travelling from bloom to bloom, they brush castaña pollen onto other castaña blossoms, fertilizing them and causing them to grow into seed pods.

Castañas support many other kinds of plants, so there are always flowers of some sort blooming on or around a wild castaña tree. These flowers attract bees. Rainforest bees are active throughout the year, and they need to find food almost every day. A steady

Many kinds of plants, including orchids (far right), grow on castaña branches. The sizes and shapes of flowers match the many kinds of bees that come to collect pollen and nectar (right). The flowers are designed to ensure that pollen gets stuck on the bees' bodies and is carried to other blossoms.

abundance of flowers — castaña blossoms, orchid flowers and other blooms — means lots of bees to feed on and pollinate the blossoms.

When people tried to grow castañas on plantations, they weren't able to imitate the rainforest. They planted row upon row of nothing but castaña trees. The trees blossomed all together and were all bare of flowers in other seasons. Bees weren't able to find food regularly on the castaña plantations, so they didn't come to feed. With no bees to pollinate the blossoms, the castañas didn't produce seed pods and nuts. Castaña plantations failed, and people learned that it takes a whole forest of flowers to make castañas possible.

People who live along the Amazon River look to the forest around them for everything they need, from foods and medicines to building materials, and the castaña harvest that brings them money from the sale of the nuts. Each tree may produce thousands of nuts, but the trees are widely scattered. The castaña collector must walk deep into the forest for many hours during the harvest. People can't collect all the castaña pods before the agoutis find them, and enough seeds are scattered to ensure that new castaña trees will grow.

Children help gather the fallen pods. Men carry huge sacks of nuts weighing more than 50 kg (100 lb) through the forest out to the rivers. The crop is carried by canoes to villages where the nuts are dried and shelled. Shelling castañas creates jobs for women in the communities along the Amazon. The best nuts sell as food, and nuts

Rainforests have many riches other than just trees for lumber. Some can be collected without destroying the forest, and also give the people who live nearby a source of income. Mayan children in Guatemala (opposite) gather allspice fruits and leaves to be sold as spices or as perfume for soaps. In Peru (right), the castaña harvest is a family affair.

that have been damaged are pressed for a rich oil that goes into soap and cosmetics. If a village gets a fair price for castaña nuts, villagers have a reason to keep the surrounding rainforest standing. In Peru, a law gives people the right to own a patch of forest to harvest castañas, preventing its destruction for lumber or to make cattle pasture. A few castaña trees can save thousands of other trees and all the life that a section of forest supports.

There is an old saying that "mighty oaks from tiny acorns grow." But the real truth is greater than this — a whole web of living relationships can sprout with the seed of a tree. Castañas help make life in the rainforest possible for orchids and pineapples, bees and frogs, rodents and peccaries and parrots, and people too.

The more we learn about the connections between plants and animals in the rainforest, the richer our lives become. We trace so many of our everyday foods, medicines, spices and materials back to the mysteries of rainforest life. Who knows how many more amazing discoveries remain to be made?

Index

JAN 2001